11+ Confide

CEM-Style Practice Exam Papers

Book

2

Copyright © Eureka! Eleven Plus Exams 2015, 2016. **Revised 28 April 2016**
Please check the website **www.eureka11plus.org/updates** for updates and clarifications to this book.
ISBN-13: 978-1514270226   ISBN-10: 1514270226

First Published in the United Kingdom by: Level 2, Eureka House, 7 Lapstone Gardens,
Eureka! Eleven Plus Exams   Harrow, Middlesex, HA3 0DZ,
Email: **office@eureka11plus.org**   United Kingdom
Fax: +44 20 8082 5109

We are all human and vulnerable to error. Eureka! Eleven Plus is very grateful to any reader who notifies us on office@eureka11plus.org of an unnoticed error, so we can immediately correct it and provide a tangible reward.

Helping your child gain confidence through practice

As the 11+ examination approaches, it is wise to practice as much as possible, but with limited time available it is equally important for the process itself to build the fund of knowledge and skills. The nature of exams is continually changing and sometimes seems deliberately obscure.

There is a trend towards multiple choice formats that are quick and cheap to mark. Pupils need experience in deciding and documenting their choices rapidly and clearly. Pupils also need familiarity with questions couched in this way. Wise parents recognise that pupils also need to focus on aspects they find difficult, and need guidance when they get stuck or make mistakes.

The *Eureka! 11+ Confidence* series of Exam Papers provides this:

- Question papers laid out in modern, multiple-choice format.
- Answer sheets laid out in modern format (in places requiring digit-by-digit entry)
- Full answers with explanations
- Supplementary books giving very detailed methods, tips and tricks on the more challenging aspects of Numerical, Non-Verbal and Verbal Reasoning

In supporting your child's preparation for the exam:

- Do as much exam paper practice as possible. The variety of material helps retain attention.
- Cut out the multiple choice answer sheet and use it to record the answers. This will reduce exam-day anxiety.
- Carry out the practice exams formally: pupil seated alone, away from *any* distractions.
- Give no help (nor encouragement) during their timed attempt at the paper.
- Immediately after the paper, encourage the pupil to mark their own work. Immediacy and involvement increase interest and enjoyment in exam preparation.
- Insist on discussing the questions which were not answered correctly. Do not set aside any errors as "silly mistakes". All mistakes are silly. The key to 11+ is attention to seemingly small details.

The gains from practice arise not only through increasing familiarity with the process, but also through enhancing the fundamental skills being tested. Underline the importance of learning how errors were made and how they may be prevented in future. Tips, tricks and (most of all) systematic approaches for avoiding the major traps at 11+ are given in the associated *"Eureka! Challenging Maths and Numerical Reasoning Exam Questions for 11+"* series of books. An efficient tool for concentrated enhancement of synonyms, antonyms, vocabulary and cloze (complete-the-sentence) is the *1000 Word Brain Boost* series. The *Non-Verbal Ninja* training course takes pupils step-by-step through the discovery of rules for the trickiest non-verbal puzzles.

Thoughtful support from parents can be crucial for pupils in the run-up to examinations. Use the Eureka! Practice Papers, with the *Numerical Reasoning* advanced training, *Brain Boost* vocabulary training books, and *Non-Verbal Ninja* training course, to help them reach their full potential.

Using this book to practice for your 11+

Make the practice as realistic as possible, to get the most benefit.

Cut out the answer sheet so that you do not have to flick back and forth.

Find a place where you will be undisturbed for 45 minutes.

Ensure the background is quiet: no TV, radio, computer, music or chat.

Do not get help or encouragement from anyone while you are doing the timed exam.

Immediately after answering the paper, mark yourself using the answers at the back.

Where you made a mistake, or got stuck, read the explanation and discuss with your parent or teacher. It may seem embarrassing to discuss a mistake but your success in 11+ depends on you thinking carefully about each mistake and improving your methods so that you make fewer in future.

Do as much exam paper practice as you can.

If you are finding it difficult to answer the Numerical Reasoning questions correctly, use the *Eureka! Maths and Numerical Reasoning* workbooks which give detailed methods, tips and tricks through worked examples on difficult questions designed to maximise your learning. Focussed training in difficult vocabulary, synonyms and antonyms can be obtained in the *1000 Word Brain Boost* training workbooks.

The instructions in an exam may be similar to those shown below. You may also get instructions played from a recording or read out. These might give you individual time limits for sections of the paper.

Instructions you may receive in the 11+ Exam

Do all your working in the question book.

Write your answers on the answer sheet, as only this will be marked.

Each paper consists of a series of sections which may have individual time limits.

Sections may begin with an example. You are free to refer back to the examples as often as you wish.

Before each section you may be told the time allowed and the number of questions in that section.

Answer as many questions as you can. If there is a question you cannot answer, move on to the next question.

There is no negative marking. Incorrect answers score nothing.

If you have time left at the end of a timed section, go back and answer any questions you have missed, but only within that same section.

Write your name:

C

Comprehension

1 Ⓐ Ⓑ Ⓒ Ⓓ
2 Ⓐ Ⓑ Ⓒ Ⓓ
3 Ⓐ Ⓑ Ⓒ Ⓓ
4 Ⓐ Ⓑ Ⓒ Ⓓ
5 Ⓐ Ⓑ Ⓒ Ⓓ
6 Ⓐ Ⓑ Ⓒ Ⓓ
7 Ⓐ Ⓑ Ⓒ Ⓓ
8 Ⓐ Ⓑ Ⓒ Ⓓ

Find the Missing Words

1 Ⓐ Ⓑ Ⓒ Ⓓ Ⓔ
2 Ⓐ Ⓑ Ⓒ Ⓓ Ⓔ
3 Ⓐ Ⓑ Ⓒ Ⓓ Ⓔ
4 Ⓐ Ⓑ Ⓒ Ⓓ Ⓔ
5 Ⓐ Ⓑ Ⓒ Ⓓ Ⓔ
6 Ⓐ Ⓑ Ⓒ Ⓓ Ⓔ
7 Ⓐ Ⓑ Ⓒ Ⓓ Ⓔ
8 Ⓐ Ⓑ Ⓒ Ⓓ Ⓔ

Analogies

1 Ⓐ Ⓑ Ⓒ Ⓓ Ⓔ
2 Ⓐ Ⓑ Ⓒ Ⓓ Ⓔ
3 Ⓐ Ⓑ Ⓒ Ⓓ Ⓔ
4 Ⓐ Ⓑ Ⓒ Ⓓ Ⓔ
5 Ⓐ Ⓑ Ⓒ Ⓓ Ⓔ
6 Ⓐ Ⓑ Ⓒ Ⓓ Ⓔ
7 Ⓐ Ⓑ Ⓒ Ⓓ Ⓔ
8 Ⓐ Ⓑ Ⓒ Ⓓ Ⓔ

Non-verbal Skills

1   Ⓐ Ⓑ Ⓒ Ⓓ Ⓔ Ⓕ
2   Ⓐ Ⓑ Ⓒ Ⓓ Ⓔ Ⓕ
3   Ⓐ Ⓑ Ⓒ Ⓓ Ⓔ Ⓕ
4   Ⓐ Ⓑ Ⓒ Ⓓ Ⓔ Ⓕ
5   Ⓐ Ⓑ Ⓒ Ⓓ Ⓔ Ⓕ
6   Ⓐ Ⓑ Ⓒ Ⓓ Ⓔ Ⓕ
7   Ⓐ Ⓑ Ⓒ Ⓓ Ⓔ Ⓕ
8   Ⓐ Ⓑ Ⓒ Ⓓ Ⓔ Ⓕ
9   Ⓐ Ⓑ Ⓒ Ⓓ Ⓔ Ⓕ
10 Ⓐ Ⓑ Ⓒ Ⓓ Ⓔ Ⓕ
11 Ⓐ Ⓑ Ⓒ Ⓓ Ⓔ Ⓕ
12 Ⓐ Ⓑ Ⓒ Ⓓ Ⓔ Ⓕ
13 Ⓐ Ⓑ Ⓒ Ⓓ Ⓔ Ⓕ
14 Ⓐ Ⓑ Ⓒ Ⓓ Ⓔ Ⓕ
15 Ⓐ Ⓑ Ⓒ Ⓓ Ⓔ Ⓕ
16 Ⓐ Ⓑ Ⓒ Ⓓ Ⓔ Ⓕ
17 Ⓐ Ⓑ Ⓒ Ⓓ Ⓔ Ⓕ

Numerical Reasoning Part A

1 Ⓐ Ⓑ Ⓒ Ⓓ Ⓔ
2 Ⓐ Ⓑ Ⓒ Ⓓ Ⓔ
3 Ⓐ Ⓑ Ⓒ Ⓓ Ⓔ
4 Ⓐ Ⓑ Ⓒ Ⓓ Ⓔ
5 Ⓐ Ⓑ Ⓒ Ⓓ Ⓔ
6 Ⓐ Ⓑ Ⓒ Ⓓ Ⓔ
7 Ⓐ Ⓑ Ⓒ Ⓓ Ⓔ
8 Ⓐ Ⓑ Ⓒ Ⓓ Ⓔ

Numerical Reasoning Part B
Write digits *and* shade the boxes

1   2   3   4   5   6   7   8

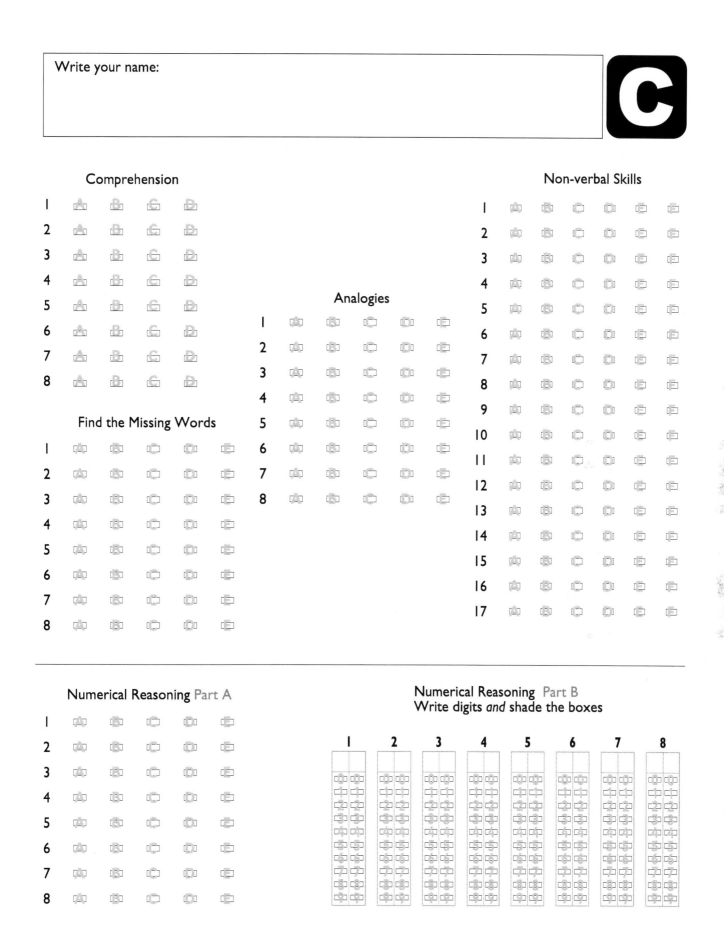

Write your name:

Comprehension

1 Ⓐ Ⓑ Ⓒ Ⓓ
2 Ⓐ Ⓑ Ⓒ Ⓓ
3 Ⓐ Ⓑ Ⓒ Ⓓ
4 Ⓐ Ⓑ Ⓒ Ⓓ
5 Ⓐ Ⓑ Ⓒ Ⓓ
6 Ⓐ Ⓑ Ⓒ Ⓓ
7 Ⓐ Ⓑ Ⓒ Ⓓ
8 Ⓐ Ⓑ Ⓒ Ⓓ

Find the Missing Words

1 Ⓐ Ⓑ Ⓒ Ⓓ Ⓔ
2 Ⓐ Ⓑ Ⓒ Ⓓ Ⓔ
3 Ⓐ Ⓑ Ⓒ Ⓓ Ⓔ
4 Ⓐ Ⓑ Ⓒ Ⓓ Ⓔ
5 Ⓐ Ⓑ Ⓒ Ⓓ Ⓔ
6 Ⓐ Ⓑ Ⓒ Ⓓ Ⓔ
7 Ⓐ Ⓑ Ⓒ Ⓓ Ⓔ
8 Ⓐ Ⓑ Ⓒ Ⓓ Ⓔ

Matching Words

1 Ⓐ Ⓑ Ⓒ Ⓓ Ⓔ
2 Ⓐ Ⓑ Ⓒ Ⓓ Ⓔ
3 Ⓐ Ⓑ Ⓒ Ⓓ Ⓔ
4 Ⓐ Ⓑ Ⓒ Ⓓ Ⓔ
5 Ⓐ Ⓑ Ⓒ Ⓓ Ⓔ
6 Ⓐ Ⓑ Ⓒ Ⓓ Ⓔ
7 Ⓐ Ⓑ Ⓒ Ⓓ Ⓔ
8 Ⓐ Ⓑ Ⓒ Ⓓ Ⓔ

Non-verbal Skills

1   Ⓐ Ⓑ Ⓒ Ⓓ Ⓔ Ⓕ
2   Ⓐ Ⓑ Ⓒ Ⓓ Ⓔ Ⓕ
3   Ⓐ Ⓑ Ⓒ Ⓓ Ⓔ Ⓕ
4   Ⓐ Ⓑ Ⓒ Ⓓ Ⓔ Ⓕ
5   Ⓐ Ⓑ Ⓒ Ⓓ Ⓔ Ⓕ
6   Ⓐ Ⓑ Ⓒ Ⓓ Ⓔ Ⓕ
7   Ⓐ Ⓑ Ⓒ Ⓓ Ⓔ Ⓕ
8   Ⓐ Ⓑ Ⓒ Ⓓ Ⓔ Ⓕ
9   Ⓐ Ⓑ Ⓒ Ⓓ Ⓔ Ⓕ
10 Ⓐ Ⓑ Ⓒ Ⓓ Ⓔ Ⓕ
11 Ⓐ Ⓑ Ⓒ Ⓓ Ⓔ Ⓕ
12 Ⓐ Ⓑ Ⓒ Ⓓ Ⓔ Ⓕ
13 Ⓐ Ⓑ Ⓒ Ⓓ Ⓔ Ⓕ
14 Ⓐ Ⓑ Ⓒ Ⓓ Ⓔ Ⓕ
15 Ⓐ Ⓑ Ⓒ Ⓓ Ⓔ Ⓕ
16 Ⓐ Ⓑ Ⓒ Ⓓ Ⓔ Ⓕ
17 Ⓐ Ⓑ Ⓒ Ⓓ Ⓔ Ⓕ

Numerical Reasoning Part A

1 Ⓐ Ⓑ Ⓒ Ⓓ Ⓔ
2 Ⓐ Ⓑ Ⓒ Ⓓ Ⓔ
3 Ⓐ Ⓑ Ⓒ Ⓓ Ⓔ
4 Ⓐ Ⓑ Ⓒ Ⓓ Ⓔ
5 Ⓐ Ⓑ Ⓒ Ⓓ Ⓔ
6 Ⓐ Ⓑ Ⓒ Ⓓ Ⓔ
7 Ⓐ Ⓑ Ⓒ Ⓓ Ⓔ
8 Ⓐ Ⓑ Ⓒ Ⓓ Ⓔ

Numerical Reasoning Part B
Write digits *and* shade the boxes

1	2	3	4	5	6	7	8

You have 45 minutes to answer the questions in this paper.

Comprehension
Read the passage below. Answer the questions by shading one of the choices A to D.

Three weeks later the world was advised of the coming of a new breakfast food, heralded under the resounding name of "Filboid Studge." Spayley, the advertising expert, put forth no pictures of massive babies springing up with fungus-like rapidity under its forcing influence, or of representatives of the leading nations of the world scrambling with fatuous eagerness for its possession. One huge sombre poster depicted the Damned in Hell suffering a new torment from their inability to get at the Filboid Studge which elegant young fiends held in transparent bowls just beyond their reach. The scene was rendered even more gruesome by a subtle suggestion of the features of leading men and women of the day in the portrayal of the Lost Souls; prominent individuals of both political parties, Society hostesses, well-known dramatic authors and novelists, and distinguished aviators were dimly recognizable in that doomed throng; noted lights of the musical-comedy stage flickered wanly in the shades of the Inferno, smiling still from force of habit, but with the fearsome smiling rage of baffled effort. The poster bore no fulsome allusions to the merits of the new breakfast food, but a single grim statement ran in bold letters along its base: "They cannot buy it now."

Spayley had grasped the fact that people will do things from a sense of duty which they would never attempt as a pleasure. There are thousands of respectable middle-class men who, if you found them unexpectedly in a Turkish bath, would explain in all sincerity that a doctor had ordered them to take Turkish baths; if you told them in return that you went there because you liked it, they would stare in pained wonder at the frivolity of your motive.

And so it was with the new breakfast food. No one would have eaten Filboid Studge as a pleasure, but the grim austerity of its advertisement drove parents in shoals to the grocers' shops to clamour for an immediate supply. In small kitchens solemn pig-tailed daughters helped depressed mothers to perform the primitive ritual of its preparation. On the breakfast-tables of cheerless parlours it was partaken of in silence. Once the womenfolk discovered that it was thoroughly unpalatable, their zeal in forcing it on their households knew no bounds. "You haven't eaten your Filboid Studge!" would be screamed at the appetiteless clerk as he hurried wearily from the breakfast-table, and his evening meal would be prefaced by a warmed-up mess which would be explained as "your Filboid Studge that you didn't eat this morning." Those fanatics who ostentatiously mortify themselves, inwardly and outwardly, with health biscuits and health garments, battened aggressively on the new food. A peer's daughter died from eating too much of the compound. A further advertisement was obtained when an infantry regiment mutinied when this new food was adopted as its breakfast fare.

Filboid Studge had become a household word, but its producer wisely realized that it was not necessarily the last word in breakfast diets; its supremacy would be challenged as soon as some yet more unpalatable food should be put on the market.

Adapted from the work of H H Munro

▶   Please continue to the next page

1   Initially, what was the main advertising theme for Filboid Studge?

A   Eating it would make babies grow faster.

B   Diplomats from many countries were eager to obtain it.

C   Not eating Filboid Studge would tend to make you go to Hell.

D   It is so desirable that being unable to have it is a punishment.

2   What did the large poster depict?

A   People who had died were being punished for not eating their Filboid Studge.

B   Notable people of the day being prevented from eating the breakfast cereal

C   Authors, novelists, musicians and comedians, amongst others, having to do heavy work.

D   Famous people being forced to eat Filboid Studge.

3   Which of these groups of people was specifically mentioned in the advertisement?

A   People whom the viewers would have recognised as having been on trial for murder

B   Well-known aeroplane pilots

C   Leaders in the business world

D   Television personalities noted for being able to convey emotion

4   What does the story specifically say about the poster?

A   It gave only sketchy details of the ingredients of the new breakfast food.

B   It listed names of famous people who recommended it.

C   It lacked any excessive praise for the breakfast food.

D   It showed children, plants and fungi grew more quickly when they consumed Filboid Studge.

▶   Please continue to the next page

5 **What does the author say Spayley has understood?**

A Turkish baths are generally considered enjoyable but people don't like admitting it.

B Even if asked in a serious manner, respectable middle-class men do not normally reveal that they attend Turkish baths.

C It is easier to persuade customers that they should do something, than that they would enjoy doing it.

D Most users of Turkish baths think the other attendees have come for frivolous reasons.

6 **How does the author say the clerk might be affected by the new breakfast cereal?**

A The clerk would be given Filboid Studge as his evening meal.

B Filboid Studge would be mixed into the warm course of his dinner.

C The clerk would be given Filboid Studge to eat before his supper.

D He would be screamed at for not having eaten Filboid Studge for breakfast and, as a punishment, not given any supper.

7 **How did the military become involved with Filboid Studge?**

A It became widely known that a group of soldiers refused to eat Filboid Studge

B Spayley published an advertisement showing a regiment of infantry eating Filboid Studge in a systematic way.

C Filboid Studge was taken on by the army and one regiment agreed to appear in a newspaper advertisement.

D Soldiers seeing the advertisement demanded to have Filboid Studge adopted as their regiment's standard breakfast food.

8 **What does the author say that Filboid Studge's producer realised?**

A A worse-tasting food might reduce the sales of Filboid Studge.

B Filboid Studge could not always be the last part of a breakfast.

C People would soon want to eat something else together with it at breakfast-time.

D If a tastier food were to arrive, Filboid Studge would no longer be the top seller.

▶ Please continue to the next page

Find the Missing Words

One or two words are missing in each sentence below. Complete the sentence by marking one of the choices A to E.

Example

A	B	C	D	E
drought	wind	rain	warm	changeable

The gentle shower of rain was very welcome after so many weeks of [Example] .

The correct answer is A. Mark it as shown below.

Question 1

A	B	C	D	E
cures	coarse	covers	course	cores

This was not the delicate, sophisticated fabric she had wanted to envelop her pillows: it was [Question 1] material with ugly stripes.

Question 2

A	B	C	D	E
hidden	hanger	arched	hangar	holding

A shaft of summer sunlight cut through the [Question 2] as its giant doors opened, revealing the top secret helicopter to the select group of military dignitaries.

▶   Please continue to the next page

Question 3

A	B	C	D	E
tale	lore	law	tail	tile

The story of the love-struck couple who eloped in a riverboat is an established part of local

| Question 3 |.

Question 4

A	B	C	D	E
halter	alter	all	altar	alder

"What's done is done, and I cannot | Question 4 | it," he confided to the priest.

Question 5

A	B	C	D	E
council	console	counsel	conceal	cancel

They were glad to receive good | Question 5 | for the difficult decision on whether to | Question 6 |
the development of the new machine after all that investment.

Questions 7 and 8

A	B	C	D	E
vein	envelop	vain	envelope	vane

Realising too late the seriousness of the warning letter she had ignored earlier, she struggled in

| Question 7 | as the fake doctor's mysterious drug flowed into her body and a warm stupor began to

| Question 8 | her.

►   Please continue to the next page

Analogies

Examine the relationship between the first pair of words. Then look at the next word and identify which of the options **A – E** produces a second pair with a relationship best matching the first. Each question has only one correct answer. For each question shade your one chosen answer on the answer sheet.

Example

Man is to woman as fox is to

A	B	C	D	E
child	boy	pregnant	mare	vixen

The correct answer is E. Mark it on the answer sheet as shown below.

Achievement is to reward as crime is to

A	B	C	D	E
loot	getaway	jewellery	penalty	capture

1

Newspaper is to read as sandwich is to

A	B	C	D	E
bread	ham	see	eaten	made

2

Europe is to Sweden as Asia is to

A	B	C	D	E
Japan	Peking	Baghdad	France	Atlantic

3

▶   Please continue to the next page

All is to many as none is to

	A	B	C	D	E
4	rarely	empty	infrequently	vanished	few

Architect is to skyscrapers as sculptor is to

	A	B	C	D	E
5	wax	statue	art	chisel	wood

Cool is to cold as old is to

	A	B	C	D	E
6	aged	oldest	historical	ancient	told

Gift is to presenting as secret is to

	A	B	C	D	E
7	concealed	fallacy	past	future	confiding

Hospital is to patients as museum is to

	A	B	C	D	E
8	dinosaurs	visitors	paintings	guides	statues

▶ Please continue to the next page

Non-verbal Reasoning

In the group of pictures on the left, one is missing.

Choose the one picture on the right that is best suited as the missing picture.

I

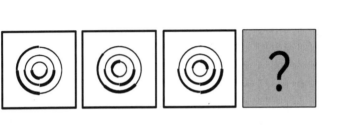

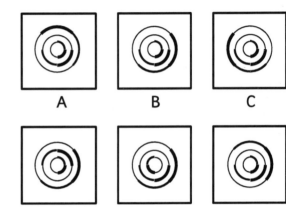

2

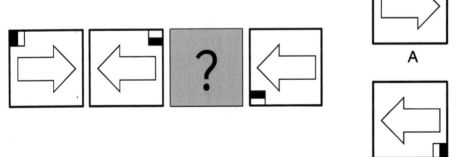

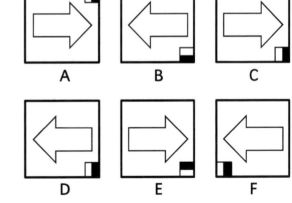

▶ Please continue to the next page

3

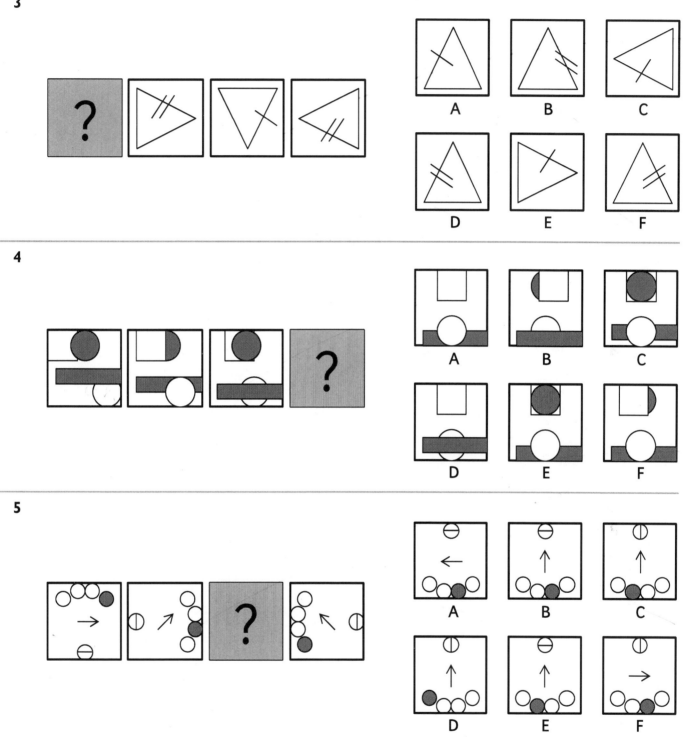

4

5

▶ Please continue to the next page

6

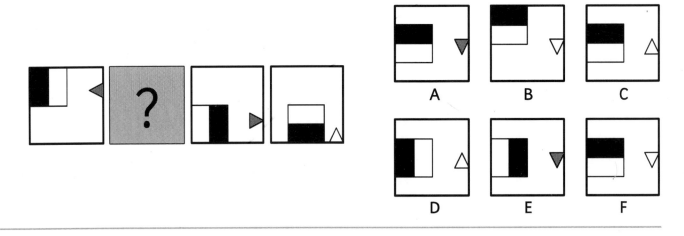

7

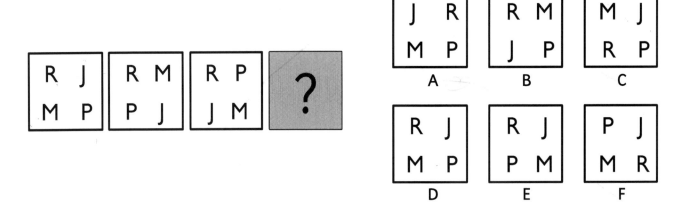

8

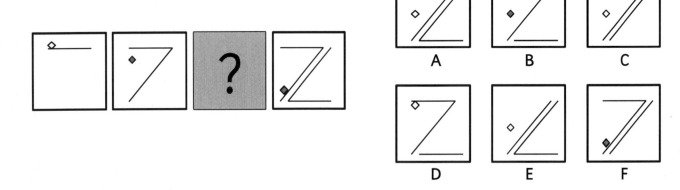

▶   Please continue to the next page

9

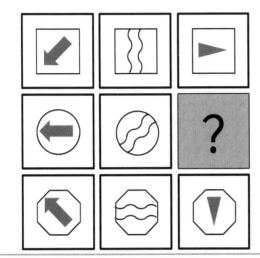

A

B

C

D

E

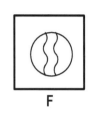
F

10

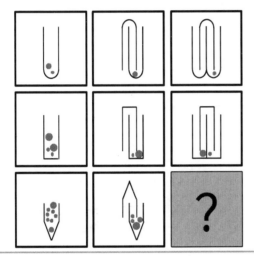

A

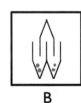
B

C

D

E

F

11

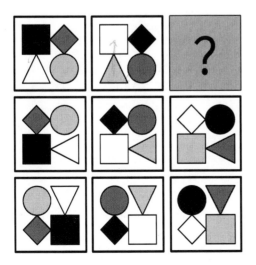

A

B

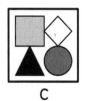
C

D

E

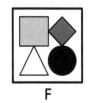
F

▶ Please continue to the next page

12

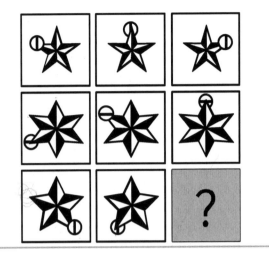

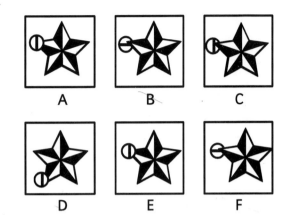

13

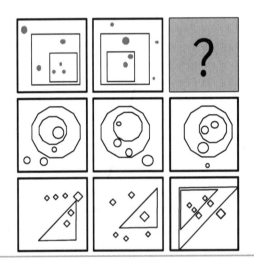

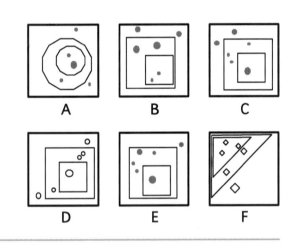

14

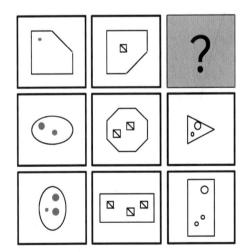

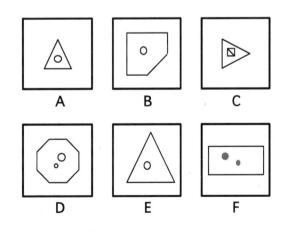

▶ Please continue to the next page

15

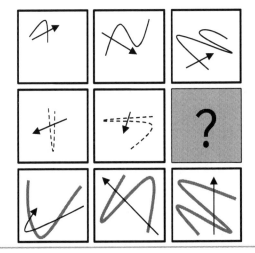 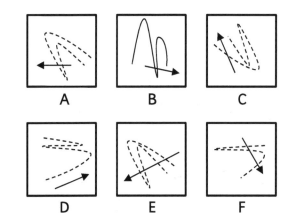

16

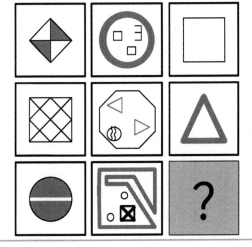 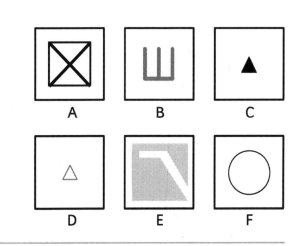

17

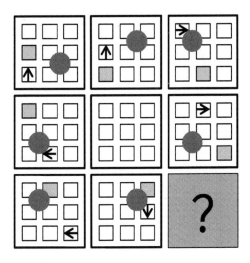 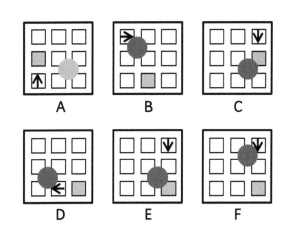

▶ Please continue to the next page

Numerical Reasoning Part A

I

Seven children pick strawberries, collecting 231 altogether. They share them equally. Three of the children are sisters, and decide to pool their strawberries to take them home in one large bag. How many strawberries will they put in that bag?

A	B	C	D	E
21	23	33	99	123

2

Alec saves £4 per week from the pocket money he receives at the end of each week. He wants to buy a model aeroplane for £70. If he starts saving now, at the start of a week, how long will it be before he has saved enough money to buy the aeroplane?

A	B	C	D	E
17	18	66	70	280

3

Which one of these three prize amounts is the median?

A	B	C	D	E
one third of one hundred pounds	1/2 of £60	a 3×3 grid of plates, each containing three £1 coins	3 £10 notes and 3 £1 coins	£8, doubled, and doubled again

4

After a wonderful restaurant meal, the three friends decided to add a generous tip to the £39 bill, so that they each contributed £17 to the total payment. How much was the tip?

A	B	C	D	E
2	12	19	20	21

▶ Please continue to the next page

5

The overnight train promised to be exciting, with a bunk bed and fancy furnishings, but how long would the journey take, if it began at 22:30 and finished at a quarter past 6 in the morning?

A	B	C	D	E
5.75 hours	6 hours	7 hours 15 min	7 1/2 hours	7 hours 45 min

6

Two hundred and fifty people squeezed into the concert hall. Half were men. Forty percent of the people bought popcorn. What is the range of possible numbers of men who bought popcorn (smallest to largest)?

A	B	C	D	E
100 to 175	75 to 125	40 to 210	125 to 150	0 to 100

"These chocolate sticks are marvellously tasty, and hardly any calories!" enthused Lucille.

"Even though it says they are 450 Calories per 100g, the box contains only 40g of them."

7

How many Calories are in one boxful of chocolate sticks?

A	B	C	D	E
40	18	180	80	45

8

"And they are a bargain," said the shopkeeper. "£0.99 per box, or £3 for 5 boxes."

How much money would Lucille save by buying the 5-box deal rather than 5 separate boxes?

A	B	C	D	E
£1.95	£2.10	£2	£2.97	£3

▶   Please continue to the next page

Numerical Reasoning Part B

Write the two digits, one in each box. Put a zero in the first box if your answer is less than 10. Shade one box in each column, corresponding to the digits.

1

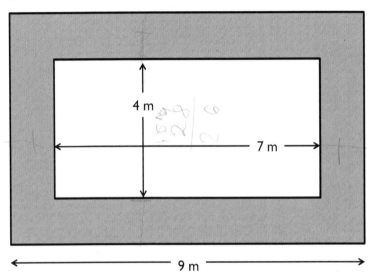

4 m

7 m

9 m

The Nawab of Shirazpur was delighted with the gigantic painting prepared for his great hall, but he also wants an enormous golden frame (shaded in this sketch) to go around it, giving an equal-sized border on all four sides.

What is the shaded area of the golden frame, in square metres?

2

Relocating the Zebulon Zoo was a traumatic task. One hundred and twenty animals remained to transport, and they belonged to five species. The numbers of three species are shown in this table.

The Giraffes outnumber the Zebras 2:1.

How many Giraffes are there?

Animal	Number
Hippopotamus	32
Zebra	
Rhinoceros	12
Giraffe	
Elephant	13

3

Farmer Nelda buys 500 kg of grain for her flock of 15 sheep. Each sheep eats 800 g of grain per day. For how many days can she fully feed her flock? (Do not count any final day where there is not enough grain to feed the whole flock).

Note:

1 kg = 1000 g   1 kilogram = 1000 grams

► Please continue to the next page

"Everyone says there's no need to practice for this exam," complained Griselda. "I don't care if I scored low on these two practice papers, it is only the real exam that counts."

"But I increased my score enormously. This could help you a lot," replied Tabitha, pressing into her best friend's reluctant hands the other practice books.

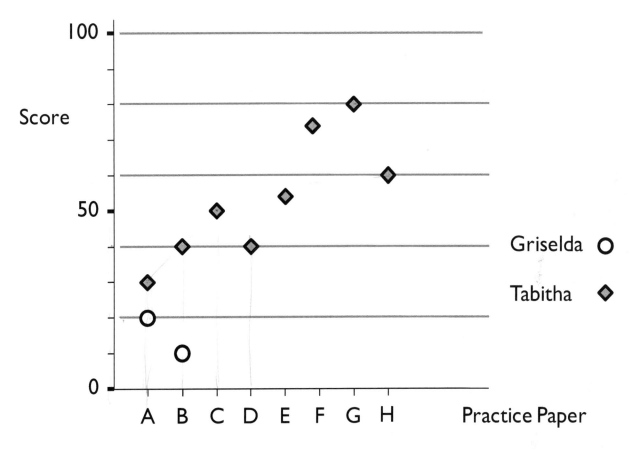

4

What was Tabitha's average score on paper C and paper D?

5

On paper A, how much higher was Tabitha's score than Griselda's?

6

If, from paper A to paper H, Griselda increases her score by the same number of points as Tabitha does, how much will Griselda score on paper H?

▶   Please continue to the next page

7

By the end of a day at the market, Violet had managed to sell all of the two dozen phone chargers at £5 each, having bought them for £3 each.

The scarves, her other product, had fared less well. She had sold only half of the dozen, at £10 each, and had to slash her price to sell the rest at £5 each, just the price she had originally paid for them.

What was her total profit that day?

8

This shape has mirror symmetry in two axes. What is its perimeter, in m?

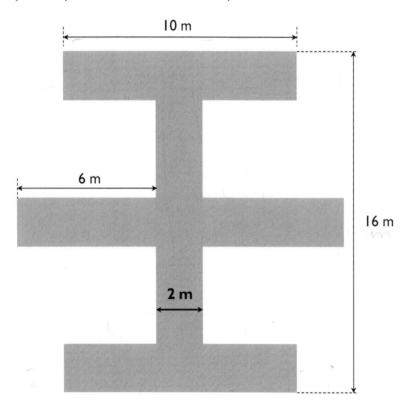

This is the end of this exam paper.

You have 45 minutes to answer the following questions.

Comprehension

Read the passage below. Answer the questions by shading one of the choices A to D.

I was so pleased at having given the slip to Long John that I began to enjoy myself and look around me with some interest on the strange land that I was in.

I had crossed a marshy tract full of willows, bulrushes, and outlandish, swampy trees; and I had now come out upon the skirts of an open piece of undulating, sandy country, about a mile long, dotted with a few pines and a great number of contorted trees, not unlike the oak in growth, but pale in the foliage, like willows. On the far side of the open stood one of the hills, with two quaint, craggy peaks shining vividly in the sun.

I now felt for the first time the joy of exploration. The isle was uninhabited; my shipmates I had left behind, and nothing lived in front of me but dumb brutes and fowls. I turned hither and thither among the trees. Here and there were flowering plants, unknown to me; here and there I saw snakes, and one raised his head from a ledge of rock and hissed at me with a noise not unlike the spinning of a top. Little did I suppose that he was a deadly enemy and that the noise was the famous rattle.

Then I came to a long thicket of these oaklike trees—live, or evergreen, oaks, I heard afterwards they should be called—which grew low along the sand like brambles, the boughs curiously twisted, the foliage compact, like thatch. The thicket stretched down from one of the knolls, spreading and growing taller as it went, until it reached the margin of the broad, reedy fen, through which the nearest of the little rivers soaked its way into the anchorage. The marsh was steaming in the strong sun, and the outline of the Spy-glass trembled through the haze.

All at once there began to go a sort of bustle among the bulrushes; a wild duck flew up with a quack, another followed, and soon over the whole surface of the marsh a great cloud of birds hung screaming and circling in the air. I judged at once that some of my shipmates must be drawing near along the borders of the fen. Nor was I deceived, for soon I heard the very distant and low tones of a human voice, which, as I continued to give ear, grew steadily louder and nearer.

This put me in a great fear, and I crawled under cover of the nearest live-oak and squatted there, hearkening, as silent as a mouse. Another voice answered, and then the first voice, which I now recognized to be Silver's, once more took up the story and ran on for a long while. I drew as close as I could manage, under the favourable ambush of the crouching trees.

Crawling on all fours, I made steadily but slowly towards them, till at last, raising my head to an aperture among the leaves, I could see clear down into a little green dell beside the marsh, and closely set about with trees, where Long John Silver and another of the crew stood face to face in conversation.

Abridged from Treasure Island, by Robert Louis Stevenson

▶ Please continue to the next page

1   **What was the narrator feeling at the start of the passage?**

A   He was pleased because he had pushed Long John down a slippery slope to give himself time to get away.

B   He was delighted because he was in unfamiliar territory and he enjoyed exploring.

C   Escaping from Long John raised his spirits so that he could take pleasure in other things.

D   He was concerned that he was in a strange area, but was hoping to meet new friends.

2   **What did he encounter as he crossed the marshy tract?**

A   There were bizarre-looking trees.

B   Amongst the foliage there were wild animals in constant movement.

C   Thick walls of willow that forced him to take a detour.

D   Here and there, pieces of open sandy country.

3   **What was the mile-long sandy area like?**

A   Composed of numerous gentle hills

B   Littered with discarded clothing

C   Watery

D   Almost impassable because of distorted, pale, trees resembling pines or willows

4   **In the third paragraph, what does the narrator think about the island?**

A   Since he had killed many people on the ship, there should be nobody alive on the island.

B   Only unintelligent, thuggish or dishonest people could have got ahead of him.

C   The island ahead contained only birds and animals.

D   He was terrified when he heard a rattlesnake.

▶   Please continue to the next page

5   **What does the narrator say about the evergreen oaks?**

    A   The leaves were widely spread out, admitting shafts of hazy sunlight.

    B   The branches had notable shapes.

    C   There was a curiously large amount of sand in the leaves, even in the tall trees.

    D   Natives of the island had used the leaves to thatch their roofs.

6   **Which of these is a true statement about the thicket?**

    A   The tallest trees were in the narrowest part.

    B   It was surrounded on all sides by a marsh of reeds.

    C   Some of its shortest trees were on a hill.

    D   It grew up to the edge of a river, in which he could see an old anchor.

7   **What was the narrator doing when squatting under the live-oak?**

    A   Putting all his effort into controlling his fear

    B   Resisting the temptation to reply

    C   Avoiding breathing if possible

    D   Concentrating on listening

8   **What was the narrator doing while Silver "took up the story and ran on for a long while"?**

    A   Planning a way to get close and ambush Silver unexpectedly.

    B   Sketching the layout of the pirates' meeting place as accurately as he could.

    C   Calculating how to separate the four pirates to make a surprise attack most effective.

    D   Using natural cover to prevent his discovery while being within earshot.

▶   Please continue to the next page

Find the Missing Words

One or two words are missing in each sentence below. Complete the sentence by marking one of the choices A to E.

Example

A	B	C	D	E
table	divide	moon	sensible	tube

That night, a bright full [Example] lit their path as they sneaked back into the forbidden garden.

The correct answer is C. Mark it as shown below.

Question 1

A	B	C	D	E
sorry	no	some	much	many

I would like to be able to give you change for the parking meter, but unfortunately I don't have [Question **1**] coins.

Question 2

A	B	C	D	E
averse	avarice	abhors	adverse	avers

Many local people were reluctant to join the search party because of [Question **2**] weather which had likely contributed to the plane crash.

▶   Please continue to the next page

Question 3

A	B	C	D	E
weeks'	week's	weeks	week	week's'

The exam is in two [Question **3**] time, so we should concentrate on practising.

Question 4

A	B	C	D	E
army	personnel	military	personal	person

It was a mistake to press the button labelled "Do Not Press", we realised, as the air filled with the thud of boots and the room was filled with armed security [Question **4**].

Questions 5 and 6

A	B	C	D	E
complete	complement	complaint	compliment	compliant

"Thank you for being [Question **5**] with our no-smoking rule," said the guide. "The smoke-free atmosphere is a perfect [Question **6**] to the clean, unornamented design of this museum."

Questions 7 and 8

A	B	C	D	E
tick	empathise	tic	sympathise	kindhearted

"I [Question **7**] with that poor boy, twitching away in fear," said the talent show judge (who had never suffered from such trouble) as she awarded him an extra mark for persevering despite his nervous [Question **8**].

▶   Please continue to the next page

Matching Words

Each question shows a word and a series of options A to E.

Identify which option is most similar in meaning to the word in the question.

Mark the answer sheet with your answer.

1   diligent

A	B	C	D	E
water	thin	careful	helpful	clean

2   infamy

A	B	C	D	E
notoriety	homely	unknown	ignorance	information

3   feral

A	B	C	D	E
wild	government	dangerous	metallic	anxious

4   predilection

A	B	C	D	E
suddenness	preference	soothsaying	decreasing	diversion

▶ Please continue to the next page

5 nuance

A	B	C	D	E
softness	never	untried	subtlety	uniqueness

6 burgeon

A	B	C	D	E
flourish	attack	doctor	request	meal

7 vanguard

A	B	C	D	E
golden	lock	bumper	vanadium	lead

8 dour

A	B	C	D	E
flap	acidic	entrance	stern	smell

▶ Please continue to the next page

Non-verbal Reasoning

In the group of pictures on the left, one is missing.

Choose the one picture on the right that is best suited as the missing picture.

1

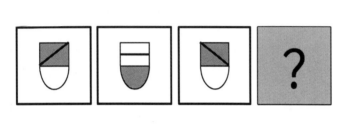 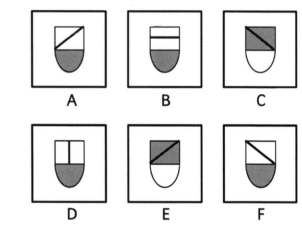

2

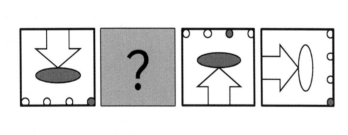 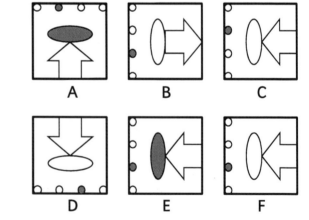

▶ Please continue to the next page

3

4

5

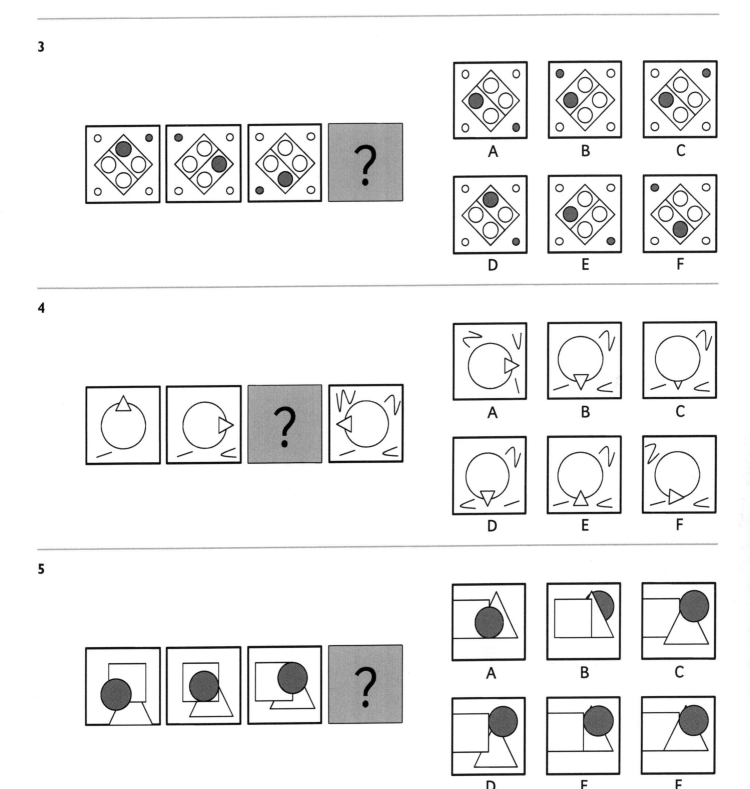

▶ Please continue to the next page

6

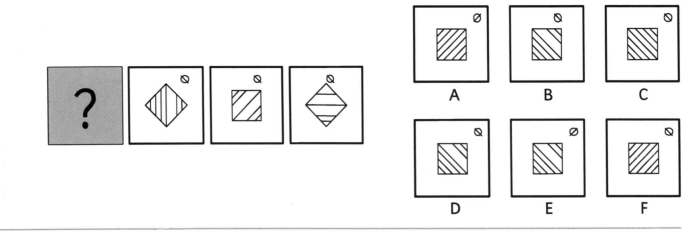

7

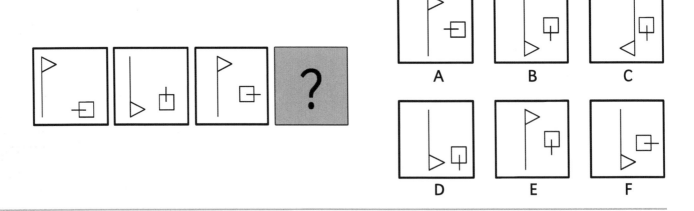

8

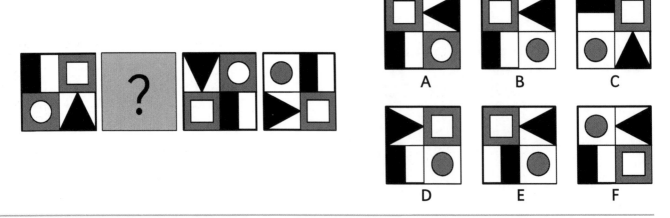

▶ Please continue to the next page

9

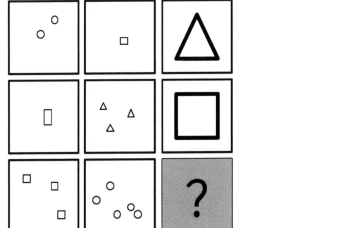 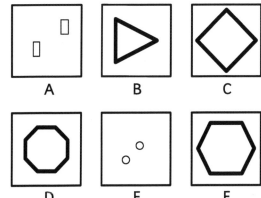

10

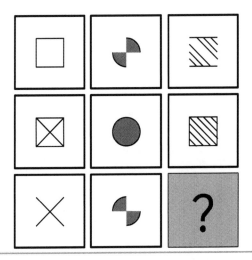 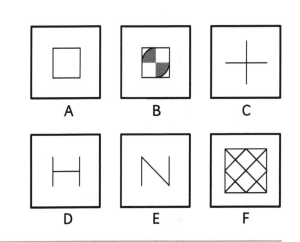

11

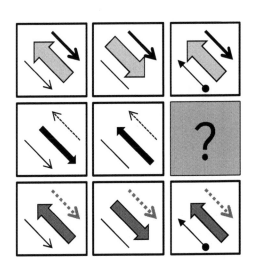 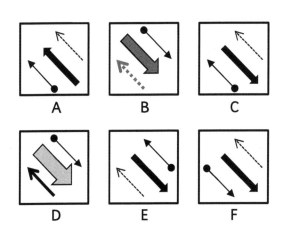

▶ Please continue to the next page

12

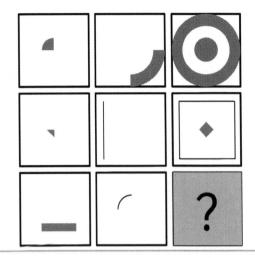
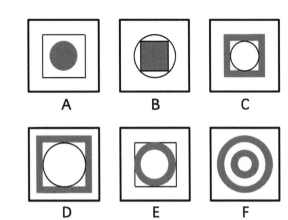

13

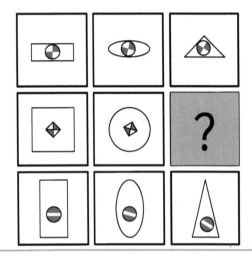
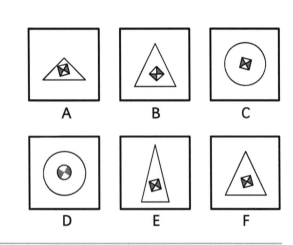

14

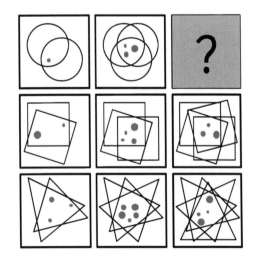
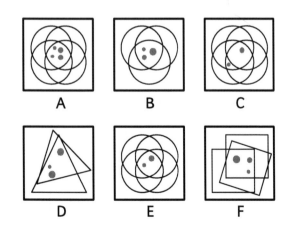

▶ Please continue to the next page

15

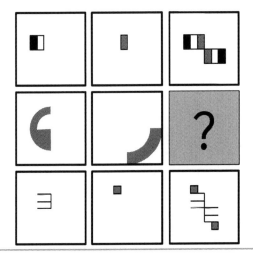 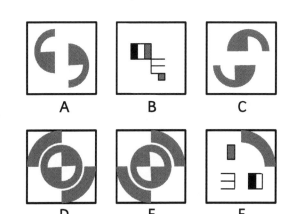

16

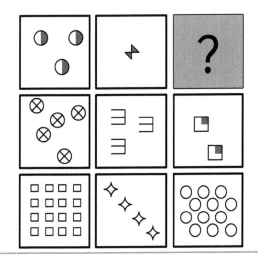 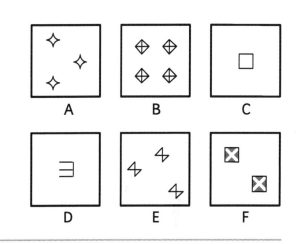

17

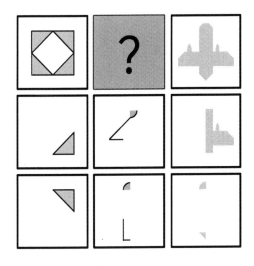 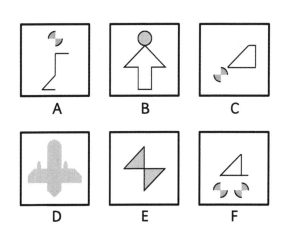

▶ Please continue to the next page

Numerical Reasoning Part A

1

Every day for two weeks, Kelly adds 15 building bricks to her model house. How many bricks did she add in total?

A	B	C	D	E
30	190	210	280	290

2

Roger manages a 400 m lap of the stadium in 2 minutes. What is his average speed in km per hour?

A	B	C	D	E
8 km/hour	12 km/hour	18 km/hour	20 km/hour	200 km/hour

Note:	
1 km = 1000 m	1 kilometre = 1000 metres

3

Of all 55 cars that passed the speed camera, 60% were speeding. Of the remainder, half were dirty. How many cars were neither speeding nor dirty?

A	B	C	D	E
11	15	22	25	33

4

To my already-bulging shopping bag weighing 5.4 kg, I add two cans of tuna that weigh 450 grams each. What does the bag now weigh?

A	B	C	D	E
5.9 kg	6.1 kg	6.3 kg	6.9 kg	9.9 kg

Note:	
1 km = 1000 m	1 kilometre = 1000 metres

► Please continue to the next page

5

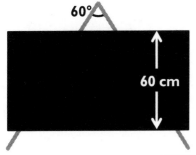

This children's blackboard has a stand (shown in grey) behind it, which is exactly as wide as the blackboard itself.

The stand is symmetrical and made of two 120 cm long wooden struts.

What is the area of the blackboard?

A	B	C	D	E
120 cm²	180 cm²	240 cm²	3600 cm²	7200 cm²

6

Nelson is filling a 20 litre tank using a 2200 ml water jug, each time having to walk to the well to fill the jug first. At the outset, the jug and the tank are empty. How many trips will he need to make to fill the tank?

A	B	C	D	E
7	8	9	10	11

Note:		
	1 l = 1000 ml	1 litre = 1000 millilitres

A car leaves St Andrews just before lunchtime at 11:13 and arrives, 77 km away at Edinburgh Airport, at 12:08. What was its average speed?

7

A	B	C	D	E
77 km/h	78 km/h	80 km/h	84 km/h	88 km/h

If it had set out at the same time but only travelled at 44 km/h, at what time would it have arrived? Give the answer in the 12-hour clock.

8

A	B	C	D	E
12:58 pm	1:13 pm	1:13 am	12:58 am	1:08 pm

▶ Please continue to the next page

Numerical Reasoning Part B

Write the two digits, one in each box. Put a zero in the first box if your answer is less than 10. Shade one box in each column, corresponding to the digits.

1

Our school's 72,000 litre swimming pool is only a quarter full this morning. If we pour in water at 1 litre per second, how many hours will it take to become full?

2

Sock colour	Number
Red	4
Blue	12
Black	24
White	8
Green	2

At my school prize-giving ceremony I am only allowed to wear white or black socks, although I have socks of many colours, as shown in this table.

What percentage of my socks are white or black?

3

Pippa is planning to pave a 1.5 metre wide, 9 metre long path in her garden. In the shop, she has now settled on beautiful beige square paving tiles that measure 50 cm on each side. How many does she need?

Note:		
	1m = 100 cm	1 metre = 100 centimetres

4

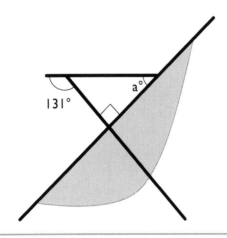

In this side view sketch of a deckchair, what is the angle a° ?

▶   Please continue to the next page

Suppose a new mathematical symbol, ❖, is introduced. It is placed between two values, and is defined to mean add the two values together and then square the result.

For example, 3 ❖ 4 = $(3+4)^2 = 7^2 = 49$.

5

What is 6 ❖ 3 ?

6

If q ❖ 7 = 400, and you know q is a positive whole number, what is q?

7

The Royal Mint reports that 3% of all pound coins in circulation are counterfeit. The pound coins collected at the school fete totalled £250 in the morning and a separate £350 in the afternoon. How many counterfeit pound coins should be expected amongst the total collection of the day?

8

The beautifully symmetrical lawn sketched here fits within a square garden, but has semicircular "bites" taken out of each side for flower beds.

What is the perimeter of the lawn?

For this question, take π to be 3.14.

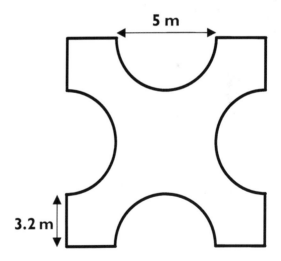

This is the end of this exam paper.

This page has been left blank intentionally.

Answers to Paper
C

Comprehension

1 **D** The Lost Souls in Hell are being punished by being able to see Filboid Studge but not quite being able to reach it.

2 **B** Some of the depicted figures resemble famous people of the day.

3 **B** Aviator means aeroplane pilot.

4 **C** "The poster bore no fulsome allusions to the merits…" Fulsome means excessive or enthusiastic.

5 **C** "People will do things from a sense of duty which they would never attempt as a pleasure," and "… would explain in all sincerity that a doctor had ordered them …" Sincerity means they would not be attempting to deceive.

6 **C** The word "prefaced" means preceded.

7 **A** The regiment mutinied (i.e. refused to follow orders) when the new breakfast was adopted, i.e. they refused to eat it. This was not an actual advertisement. Rather, the event became widely known and so acted as an advertisement.

8 **A** It is unpalatable, i.e. horrible-tasting, and its supremacy (top-selling status) might be challenged by an even more unpalatable newcomer.

Find the Missing Words

1 **B** Coarse means thick or unrefined.

2 **D** An aircraft is stored in a hangar, while clothes hang on a hanger.

3 **B** Lore means the accumulated knowledge or beliefs held by a group about a subject

4 **B** Alter means change, while an altar is a table in a church.

5 **C** Counsel is advice or to advise.

6 **E** Cancel is to decide or announce that an event won't happen, or to neutralise the effect of something. A council is a group of people.

7 **C** In vain means unsuccessfully, a vein is a blood vessel, and a vane indicates wind direction.

8 **B** Envelope is a noun. Envelop is a verb meaning to surround.

Analogies

1	**D**	Although a getaway, capture and a penalty can all follow a crime, it is the penalty that corresponds most closely to how a reward is the consequence of an achievement.
2	**D**	A newspaper is consumed by being read. Similarly, a sandwich is consumed by being eaten.
3	**A**	Sweden is a country (not a city) in Europe; therefore you must choose a country in Asia, of which only Japan is available.
4	**E**	Many is a slightly weaker form of all. Similarly, rarely is a weaker form of never. Many/all relate to proportions of items, while rarely/never relate to how often something happens.
5	**C**	An architect builds skyscrapers (in the plural), indicating it is not a single item but a habit of making many items fitting the description. Therefore you must choose something that could be multiple items, i.e. Art, which can apply to multiple statues. **Tip:** When more than one option seems to fit, look carefully at singular versus plural.
6	**D**	Cold is a more intense form of cool. Similarly, only ancient is an intensification of old.
7	**A**	The process of giving a gift is called presenting. The process of telling a secret is called confiding.
8	**B**	A hospital is for the benefit of patients, and a museum is for the benefit of visitors. **Tip:** When the most obvious link, e.g. "hospital contains patients", leads to several options seeming to fit, look for a more specific link.

Non-verbal Reasoning

1	**B**	There are three rings. Their position can be detected because in each case the line thickness varies from thin to thick around the circumference. The inner ring is rotating clockwise 90 degrees per step. The outer ring is rotating anticlockwise slower (45 degrees per step). The intermediate ring is not rotating.
2	**C**	The arrows are alternating in direction. The small black-and-white square is moving clockwise but its orientation is rotating anticlockwise.
3	**A**	The triangle is rotating clockwise. The lines crossing its wall are alternating in number between 1 and 2, and their position follows its rotation.
4	**A**	At the top, the disc is keeping still while the white square moves right, alternately in front of and behind the disc. At the bottom, the dark bar moves progressively down while the disc moves progressively left; the alternate between front and back position.
5	**B**	The arrow is rotating anticlockwise, one-eighth of a turn on each occasion. The pattern of circles is rotating clockwise each turn, and their shading is moving one position anti-clockwise with every step.
6	**F**	The black-and-white square is moving around the inside of the outer square anticlockwise, half a side at a time, while rotating about its own axis clockwise. The triangle is moving downwards, rotating anticlockwise and alternating in colour.
7	**D**	The M, J and P move in a circuit by one place each step.

8   C   The Z shape in the 4th box is being built up step by step. Although the final two steps are the addition of the second diagonal and the lower horizontal, we cannot tell which should occur in the 3rd box and which should only occur in the 4th box. We therefore have to rely on the falling diamond, which alternates in colour.

9   C   The outer element is consistent for each row. For each column, the inner element rotates clockwise 45 degrees in each step from top to bottom.

10   B   In each row, from left to right an extra piece of the background structure is added, identical to the first, either inverted or the correct way up and touching the first. In each column, the number of particles doubles with each step down.

11   D   In each column, the design rotates clockwise from top to bottom. In each row, the shapes remain unmoved but the colour scheme rotates clockwise from left to right.

12   A   In each row, the star reflects left to right from one panel to the next. The small round element moves position by one point of the star clockwise, alternating between being in front of the star and behind.

13   C   In each panel, there are two large shapes that divide the panel into three zones: outside the outer shape, between the shapes, and inside the inner shape. In the left panel, each zone contains one or more small elements. In the middle panel, whatever was in the outer zone moves to the middle zone; whatever was in the middle zone moves to the inner zone; and whatever was in the inner zone moves to the outer zone. This process happens again in the formation of the right panel.

14   A   The outer element of each of the four corner tiles is rotated right to make the outer element of the corresponding edge tile one position clockwise. The inner elements increase in number within each column from 1 at the top to 3 at the bottom.

15   A   Within each row, from left to right, the number of bends in the main curve increases by 1. Within each column, the arrow crosses the main curve once in the top cell, twice in the middle cell and three times in the lower cell.

16   F   In each row, the element in the right cell appears twice in miniature in the middle cell (rotated left and rotated right), together with another small element, and within a large element. The element in the left cell is not related to the other two cells.

17   C   As your eye passes clockwise, the grey square moves anticlockwise and the arrow moves clockwise (rotating when it reaches a corner). Meanwhile the grey disc moves anticlockwise.

Numerical Reasoning Part A

1   D   Each child's share is $231 \div 7 = 33$. Three children's share totals $33 \times 3 = 99$.

2   B $70 \div 4 = 17$ remainder 2. He will not have enough after 17 weeks: he needs 18.

3   E   They are, respectively, £33 1/3, £30, £27, £33, and £32. Arranged in order of size, £32 would be in the middle (median).

4   B $17 \times 3 = 51$. $51 - 39 = 12$.

5   E   To midnight it is 1h 30m; after that it is 6h 15m more. Total is therefore 7h 45m.

6 E   125 were men. 40%, i.e. 4/10×250 = 4×25 = 100, bought popcorn. The lowest number of men buying popcorn would be 0, if the 100 popcorn buyers were all women. The highest would be 100, if they were all men.

7 C   Tip: To calculate this efficiently and accurately without having to write out detailed multiplication or division, remember to cancel. The box is 40/100 of 450g = 4/10×450 = 4×45 = 2×90 = 180.

8 A   Separately, they would cost 5×£0.99 = £4.95. The saving is £4.95 − £3 = £1.95.

Numerical Reasoning Part B

1 26   You could break the grey area into four rectangles, calculate the area of each, and then add them up, but this involves four multiplications and is therefore prone to error. This question is more easily answered by calculating the outer area and subtracting the inner area. At the bottom, the 9 m outer border is 2 m longer than the 7 m inside border. Since the margin is the same all the way round, the outer border at the sides must be longer by the same amount, 2 m, and must therefore have length = 4+2 = 6 m. Shaded area = 9×6 − 7×4 = 54 − 28 = 26 m².

2 42   Zebras + giraffes must bring the total up to 120, so their total number is 120−(32+12+13) = 120−57 = 63. This is made up of giraffes 2 parts + zebra 1 part. To find out how many is 1 part, divide 63 by the total number of parts (3): 63÷3 = 21. Giraffes are 2 parts, i.e. 2×21 = 42.

3 41   Decide whether to use kg or g. Using g would give huge numbers (such as 500,000 g), so try kg. Per day, feed eaten by whole flock = 15 × 0.8 kg = 12 kg. Days lasted = 500÷12 = 250/6 = 125/3 (if you cancel like this, the division becomes less error-prone) = 41 2/3.

4 45   Average = (50+40)÷2=90÷2 = 45.

5 10   Difference = 30−20 =10.

6 50   Tabitha increases her score from 30 to 60, i.e. by +30. Griselda starts at 20, and will therefore (if this happens) finish with 20+30 = 50.

7 78   Profit on phone chargers = (£5 − £3) × 24 = 2×24 = £48. Profit on scarves = (£10−£5) × 6 = 5 × 6 = £30. Total 48 + 30 = £78.

8 92   The vertical segments add up to 16 m on the left half of the diagram, and another 16 m on the right half, totalling 32 m. There are horizontals at 6 levels. The topmost is 10m. The next is in two parts totalling 10−2 = 8. The third is 6+6 =12 m. The remainder are mirror images of these, so the total of the horizontal segments is 2×(10+8+12) = 2×30 = 60 m. Total = 32 + 60 = 92 m.

Answers to Paper D

Comprehension

1   **C**   It was because he had given John the slip (i.e. escaped) that he could enjoy other things.

2   **A**   Outlandish means bizarre.

3   **A**   Undulating means wave-like or gently hilly.

4   **C**   Dumb brutes means unspeaking animals; fowl means birds.

5   **B**   The boughs (which means branches) were curiously twisted.

6   **C**   It "spread down from one of the knolls (hills) … growing taller as it went".

7   **D**   Hearkening is listening.

8   **D**   The ambush from the crouching trees is a metaphor: they are surrounding him, providing convenient natural cover.

Find the Missing Words

1   **E**   Much is used with singular nouns, such as hair, water, time, money, work, and help. Many is used with plural nouns.

2   **D**   Averse means having a dislike of something. Adverse means obstructive, unfavourable or harmful. Avers means states emphatically that something is true.

3   **A**   It is a time of two weeks, which is why we write "weeks' time".

4   **B**   Personnel is a noun for a group of staff. Personal is an adjective, meaning private or relating to one individual.

5   **E**   Compliant means obedient, while complaint means objection or statement that something is unsatisfactory.

6   **B**   A complement means a suitable fit, for example between two pieces in a jigsaw. A compliment is praise.

7   **D**   You can empathise with someone going through the same emotions as you did in the past, most commonly because you had the same experience.

You can sympathise with anyone if you feel sorrow or pity for their situation: there is no need for you to have been in the same situation in the past.

8   **C**   A tic is a habitual twitch, particularly if it occurs in response to anxiety. A tick is a

mark drawn to indicate an answer is correct, or a small insect, or the sound of a clock.

Matching Words

1	**C**	Diligent means showing care in one's work.
2	**A**	Infamy is being famous for a bad feature.
3	**A**	Feral means wild or seeming to be wild.
4	**B**	Predilection means preference.
5	**D**	A subtle difference in or shade of meaning
6	**A**	Burgeon means grow or flourish, and be increasing in size or importance.
7	**E**	The vanguard is the front part of an army or group: the part that leads the way. Vanadium is a metal.
8	**D**	Dour means severe, stern or lacking in enthusiasm.

For **synonyms, antonyms, vocabulary and cloze**, the *1000 Word Brain Boost* series of workbooks provide intensive training.

Non-verbal Reasoning

1	**D**	The upper and lower regions of the shield are alternating in colour. The bar in the upper half of the shield is coloured black or white, always contrasting with that region of the shield, and is rotating slowly (1/8 of a turn per step) clockwise.
2	**F**	The entire pattern is rotating clockwise with each step. The dark colouring on one small circle is moving from one to the other in the same direction of motion. The centre oval is alternating in colour.
3	**E**	The small dark circle is moving anticlockwise. The large dark circle is moving clockwise. The diagonal line is alternating in direction.
4	**B**	The triangle moves clockwise around the big circle, and in front of (i.e. overlapping) it, while itself rotating clockwise (and therefore always pointing outwards). The squiggles build up gradually and stay in the same position once they appear.
5	**E**	Layers: The disc is at the front (never overlapped) and the triangle is at the back (always overlapped). Positions: The triangle is moving up, the square left and the disc upwards and to the right.
6	**C**	The square is rotating slowly (one-eighth of a turn per move) clockwise and losing bars from its interior. The small circle is moving slowly left, with its bar remaining in the same orientation.
7	**B**	The flag is moving right, and inverting vertically at each step. The square with a short

line extending from it is moving up and the position of the line is rotating clockwise.

8 **B** The overall shape is rotating anticlockwise. However, the square (divided into black and white halves) is retaining its orientation. The disc and small square surrounding it are alternating in colour.

9 **D** For each row, the total number of elements in the left and middle panels is the number of sides of the shape in the right panel.

10 **E** In the middle row, each panel is composed of the combination of the contents of the corresponding panels in the top and bottom rows.

11 **C** Each panel is composed of three elements: top (located at top-right), middle, and bottom (located at bottom left). The top elements are consistent within each row; the bottom elements are consistent within each column. The middle elements are consistent in shape within each row but alternate in direction.

12 **C** In each row, the design in the left panel is replicated in all 4 rotational positions within the outer square, as is the design in the middle panel, to make the right panel.

13 **F** In each column, the outer shape becomes taller and narrower from top to bottom. In each row, the inner shape rotates clockwise very slightly from left to right.

14 **E** In each row the number of large outline shapes increases by one from left to right. In each column the number of small shaded discs increases by one from top to bottom. The small shaded discs are always in the area where all the outline shapes overlap.

15 **D** In each row, the element on the left, duplicated with an 180 degree rotation, plus the element in the middle, also duplicated with an 180 degree rotation, gives the element on the right.

16 **F** The number of elements in the right column is always the number in the left column, minus the number in the middle column.

17 **B** The elements in middle and bottom cells of each column are combined, and then duplicated by reflection in the vertical midline, to make the top cell.

Numerical Reasoning Part A

1 **C** Two weeks is 14 days. $14 \times 15 =$ (by mental arithmetic) $140 + 70 = 210$.

2 **B** 400 m in 2 minutes. In one hour (60 minutes, i.e. 30 times longer), distance would be $400 \times 30 = 12000$ m $= 12$ km.

3 **A** The fraction not speeding is $40\% = 4/10 = 2/5$. $2/5 \times 55 = 2 \times 11 = 22$. Half are dirty, so the number of non-dirty non-speeding cars is 11.

4 **C** $5.4 + (2 \times 0.45) = 5.4 + 0.9 = 6.3$ kg

5 **E** Since the triangle has one angle of 60° and it is symmetrical, it is an equilateral triangle. Therefore the gap between the two free ends of the stand is also 120 cm. The blackboard is therefore 120 cm wide. It is 60 cm tall. Area $= 120 \times 60 = 7200$

cm².

6   **D**   20000÷2200 = 200/22 = 100/11 = 9 1/11. Nine trips is nearly enough but not actually enough, so he will need to make 10 trips.

7   **D**   Speed = distance ÷ time = 77 km ÷ 55 min = 7/5 km/min = 7/5×60 km/h = 7×12 km/h = 84 km/h.

8   **A**   Time = distance ÷ speed = 77÷44 = 7/4 = 1 3/4 hour = 1 hour 45 min. 11:13 + 01:45 = 12:58. This is after noon (12:00) and therefore in the 12 hour clock it is shown as p.m.

Numerical Reasoning Part B

1   **15**   1 litre/second = 3600 litres per hour. Volume to fill = 3/4 × 72,000 = 54,000 L. Time = 54,000÷3,600 = 540/36 = (cancelling by 2) 270/18 = (cancelling by 9) 30/2 = 15. **Tip**: you may at first have planned to calculate 54000÷3600 by long division, but it is sometimes easier to avoid mistakes in divisions if you do any simple cancellations. (See *Eureka! Maths and Numerical Reasoning* books for advice on making seemingly difficult questions easy.)

2   **64**   White or black: 8+24=32. Total number of socks = 50. Percentage = 32/50×100 = 32×2 = 64%.

3   **54**   **Tip**: if you have a rectangular space to tile, it sometimes avoids decimals or very large numbers to immediately calculate how many tiles fit along its length and breadth.

          Answer: Tiles along length = 9/0.5 = 18. Tiles along width = 1.5/0.5 = 3. Total number of tiles = 18 × 3 = 54.

4   **41**   The angle adjacent to 131° is 180–131 = 49°. Since the angles inside a triangle must add up to 180° and 90° is already accounted for in the right angle at the bottom, what remains, 49 + a, must add up to 90. Therefore a = 90–49 = 41.

5   **81** $(6+3)^2 = 9^2 = 81$.

6   **13** $(q+7)^2 = 400$ means q+7 = 20, so q =13.

7   **18**   3% of £600: 1% is £6, so 3% is £18.

8   **57**   There are 8 short straight sides of 3.2 m, totalling 8×3.2 = 25.6 m. There are 4 semicircular sides, equalling two circles of circumference 3.14×5 m, totalling 2×5×3.14 = 10×3.14 = 31.4 m. Perimeter = 25.6 + 31.4 = 57 m.

Printed in Great Britain
by Amazon